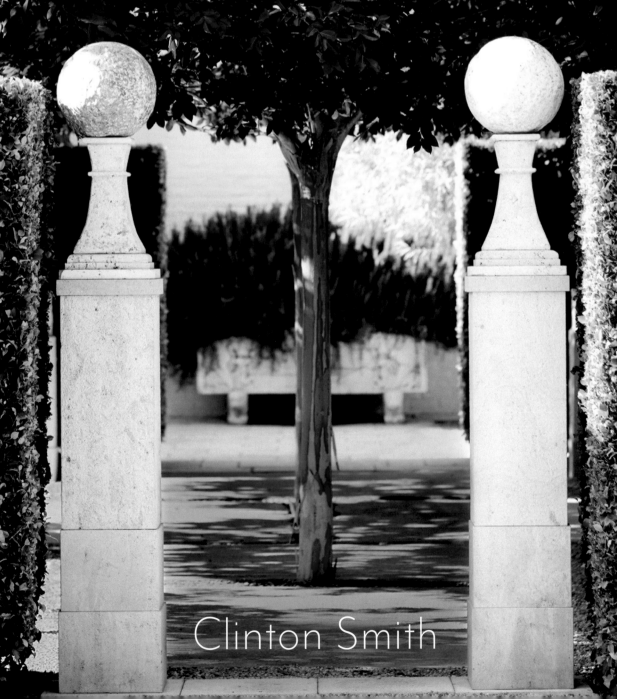

VERANDA

ESCAPES

Clinton Smith

VERANDA

ESCAPES

ALLURING OUTDOOR STYLE

Clinton Smith

HEARST
books

Ah, the great outdoors. The mix of fresh air, sunshine, and glorious, ebullient gardens is an elixir for the soul. Whether it's a humble, wildflower-edged path or an elaborate poolside veranda designed for hosting dinner under the stars, there's a world of knowledge to be found both in natural beauty as we find it, as well as in how nature is sculpted and tamed into beautiful outdoor spaces for real-life living. Enjoy this book's abundance of inspiration, as well as the Vitamin D from sunshine-filled days in your own garden. Just don't forget the SPF.

lush
landscapes

A garden is the ultimate fantasy—a verdant journey into nature's bounty and beauty. Whether meticulously pruned or wild and unrestrained, the joyous abundance of these leafy, lively retreats enchants and delights.

Preceding pages: A jasmine-laden arbor provides a fragrant backdrop in Oprah Winfrey's rose garden.
Opposite page: Koko Loko is Winfrey's favorite rose.

IN FULL BLOOM
In the hills of Montecito, Oprah Winfrey has created a lush rose garden that's a sensual, spiritual escape.

When Oprah Winfrey bought her 65-acre Montecito, California, property in 2001, she hadn't a clue about roses. "What did I know about a garden?" says the television personality and media powerhouse. "I would leave my Chicago apartment at 5:30 in the morning and come back at 8:30 at night, when it was dark. I couldn't understand what everyone was so crazy about." By everyone, Winfrey means her new neighbors in the sun-kissed coastal enclave east of Santa Barbara, where the flowers are a local obsession and the halcyon days make for a blooming season that lasts nearly all year. She discovered that acreage on her land had been set aside for roses, although none had been planted yet. "I thought, Oh boy, what am I going to do with that?" she confesses. Still, she forged ahead, turning to master rosarian Dan Bifano to create her field of flowers.

Bifano, no stranger to boldface names (he has designed gardens for Barbra Streisand and Tom Ford), showed up to their first meeting with a pail filled with blossoms so he could gauge Winfrey's taste. He then devised a scheme that incorporated her favorites, including the peachy Bronze Star, Heaven on Earth in blushing pinks, and bronze-and-lavender Distant Drums. And with Bifano as her guide, Winfrey got down into the dirt. She helped with everything from laying out flower arrangements to placing plants in the ground. "I'm very hands-on," she says. "I picked the gravel and the grout between the stonework. I decided which way the roses would face. Love is in the details."

The garden overlooks the Pacific Ocean and the Channel Islands in the distance, a picturesque vista that Winfrey and Bifano improved upon by creating a formal plan that accentuates the majestic backdrop. "I've done many interviews with people who had to lose what they had in order to value what they still have," she says. "Sometimes I stand under the arbor, close my eyes, and allow myself to take in as much as I can: I hear birds splashing in the fountain and literally smell the roses. This garden makes me present."

Opposite page: Romantic beds of roses are underplanted with dahlias, lilies, narcissi, daffodils, irises, and blooming annuals and perennials to provide year-round color. *Following pages:* Arbors dripping with Sombreuil and Pandora roses provide shade and harbor an outdoor dining area; a 19th-century cast-iron fountain gurgles in the center of the garden.

This page: For an additional note of fragrance under the arbor, Bifano mixed *Jasminum tortuosum* with the roses. *Opposite page:* Distant Drums, Elina, and Brass Band range from beige and yellow to variegated orange for a painterly effect. *Following pages:* Pathways of crushed granite are edged with matching stonework to create a neutral frame that serves to emphasize the blooms.

PICTURE PERFECT A family's California seaside getaway exudes a delightfully unplugged ambience.

After 25 years and with their children grown, one California couple looked to designer Mark Sikes for a refresh of their getaway house on the ocean in Montecito—their respite from their workaday life in Pacific Palisades. Sikes, a consummate host who exudes California cool, has a well-known affinity for outdoor spaces: indoor-outdoor living is de rigueur at his own Mediterranean-style home in the Hollywood Hills, where the windows and doors are always kept open. Here, he transformed the space into a retreat that makes entertaining guests a breeze—and encourages relaxation in general, too. The outdoor spaces did not escape his purview—poolside chaises with cheerful striped cushions add a welcoming note to the formal Spanish-Mediterranean architecture, while fire pits grace the newly enlarged patio to encourage chilly-evening conversations.

21

Opposite page: The home's elegant motor court elevates the sense of arrival. The Pacific Ocean can be seen in the distance through the doors. *Following pages:* In the backyard, Sikes balanced stately architectural elements with a graceful, barefoot vibe. "This home defines my style," he says. "It's California elegance: casual, livable, timeless."

This page: Clipped hedges line the paths of the property's beguiling rose garden, which radiates around a classical fountain.

"This home defines my style," Sikes says.
"It's California elegance: casual, livable, timeless."

FORCE OF NATURE Nestled between mountains and the Pacific Ocean, a California home is inspired by its majestic coastal setting.

The Southern California coast is no less astonishing in its beauty than it is inspiring in art and craft. The region has been home to painters, poets, architects—and interior designers like Christina Rottman, a California native who has made the seaside city of Santa Barbara her picturesque base. But when clients invited her to take a look at their house in Montecito, perched above the azure waves of the Pacific and surrounded by lofty cypress, sinewy oaks, and native succulents, even Rottman felt its unique pull. The house—designed by the revered Santa Barbara architect Bob Easton, with landscape design by Douglas Hoerr that extends the home's living space—nestles into the mountain and becomes part of the surroundings. "It's as though the property has a life force," Rottman says, "and it comes into the house."

Opposite page: A contemporary steel-cased door reveals an outdoor oasis that's as equally sleek.

This page: Wrought-iron chaises overlook a cactus garden. *Opposite page:* Poolside seating offers a commanding view of the landscape. *Following pages:* A shaded window seat is a welcoming perch in the entry courtyard.

"When we first entered the courtyard and walked up
to the front door, I was struck by the feeling that
I was suspended over the ocean," says the wife.
"It is wonderful to feel so connected to the earth."

FRENCH ACCENT Infused with the colors and patterns of the South of France, a Los Angeles estate mixes high design with a soupçon of fun.

The project began, as many do, with the renovation of a house, this one in sunny Southern California. But in the hands of Anthony Baratta and his former partner, William Diamond, as well as architect Steve Giannetti and landscape architect Perry Guillot, it then expanded to include a handful of especially unusual spaces and outbuildings: an ethereal dining pavilion, for instance; a party-ready porte cochere; a vine-wrapped poolside pergola—cum—screening room; and, in the garden, a freestanding kitchen that happens to look like a greenhouse. "When we started, we were thinking we wanted the house to be great for a wedding," says the wife. But what the homeowners, transplanted New Yorkers with three grown children, wound up with is so much more.

Baratta describes the resulting West Coast château as an "over-the-top palace in Provence." The style is Louis XV, but like Baratta himself, it bubbles with a kind of Italian joie de vivre. A virtual river of blues wends its way through the house and spills out onto the chef d'oeuvre of the manicured grounds, from the cozy blues of the loggia to the effervescent blues of the tiled pavilion. Party sites abound, but the dazzler is the fanciful, functional pavilion, inspired by the Tartar Tent at Château de Groussay. Just next door is the garden kitchen, a handsome structure that's been professionally equipped for cooking demonstrations and visiting chefs—all of which came in handy when they finally had that long-awaited wedding.

Opposite page: The dining pavilion is a French-inspired fantasy in blue and white.

This page: The cheery loggia has a relaxed Provençal charm. *Opposite page:* The tiled pavilion was inspired by a folly at a French château, but has been neatly Americanized with mini-pleated gingham lampshades and partially upholstered chair frames.

This page: Wisteria climbs a garden arbor. *Opposite page:* A collection of antique finials lines the porte cochere. Cypress trees surrounding the outdoor kitchen evoke the South of France. *Following pages:* Impeccably clipped spheres of holly frame the pool area.

*The West Coast estate evokes
the light and charm of Provence,
but with an unmistakable
Southern California joie
de vivre.*

AMERICAN BEAUTY On Long Island's fabled North Shore, the joys of country life and cosmopolitan comfort come together in style.

The long search for an idyll ended when a Manhattan couple found this 1917 getaway home on Long Island's North Shore. "They wanted a really old house that had been there forever," says designer Frank de Biasi, "but they also wanted to freshen it up." With the help of architect Leonard Woods, de Biasi added creature comforts galore—but most of that effort isn't apparent. "Behind the scenes, it's quite the modern house," he says, "but you'd never know it."

The young family of five (plus three pooches) come often, virtually every weekend and all summer, too, to their shingled white Colonial. Here, they garden and play and most of all entertain—but their style does not involve engraved invitations or uplifted pinkies at tea. "We're quite casual," says the wife, "with kids running around and dogs lying on the couches." And with six verdant acres to explore, artfully orchestrated by landscape design firm Innocenti & Webel, there's plenty of room to roam—and relax.

Opposite page: Serene sky-blue shutters adorn the facade of the 1917 home on Long Island's North Shore.

The owners wanted the home
to feel original and timeworn,
and even the landscaped spaces
conjure a bygone era.

This page: The lush grounds include a greenhouse for growing orchids and a small equipment shed inspired by structures at Colonial Williamsburg in Virginia. *Opposite page:* Shapely metal garden furniture is arranged for casual entertaining on a bluestone patio. Potted alliums line a garden walkway. *Following pages:* Stone steps articulate a gently sloping grassy allée.

ESTATE OF GRACE An enchanting garden weaves woodland magic amid the rolling Connecticut landscape.

Twenty years ago, Fred Landman asked landscape architect Charles Stick to transform the rocky, rolling topography of his Greenwich, Connecticut, estate. Inspired by their travels to legendary gardens all over the world, the duo—now dear friends—have created a verdant, meandering retreat. "The contrast between these purposefully formed man-made shapes and the surrounding woodland gives this garden a very special quality," Stick says. "My measure of a good book is that it contains something that makes me want to read another book—that curiosity is what I hope a garden like this fosters in someone's life."

A wide stone walkway unfolds, forming the backbone of the garden; the other paths act as offshoots, offering entrée into the wonderful crooks and hollows of the 14-acre property. The meandering path reveals a Ming dynasty dog statue surrounded by a cluster of boxwoods, as well as spherical junipers and false cypress that are trained by hand using a Japanese method called cloud pruning. Elsewhere, a Japanese spirit walk winds through the native forest, and a fanciful Chinese pavilion topped with a gilded pineapple occupies an island that is accessible by stepping-stones—the perfect spot for tea in the late afternoon as the sunlight bounces between the koi pond and the gold-leafed ceiling.

Closer to the house, curving European hornbeam hedges, punctuated by a row of neatly manicured linden trees, lead to a limestone statue of Atlas. Nearby, a sculpture by the legendary French artist Aristide Maillol perches on a rocky knoll, surrounded by a crush of blooming hostas. In the orchard, English bluebells burst from woven willow hurdles at the foot of apple, pear, and plum trees. Statuary and architectural stone ornaments act as guides throughout the property. "A successful garden makes you want to move through the landscape, and a well-placed ornament has a great power to achieve that, leading you to the next discovery," Stick says.

Opposite page: Antique garden statuary guides visitors through the garden.

This page: A waterfall cascades from the grotto into a rivulet lined with hostas and swamp azaleas; the large rock formation, original to the property, is a stunning backdrop to the man-made elements. *Opposite page:* The lacquered Chinese pavilion is an enticing folly.
Following pages: An undulating allée of European hornbeam hedges and linden trees lead to a towering limestone statue of Atlas.

This page: Bluebells add a flash of color at the feet of the orchard's fruit trees. *Opposite page:* Atop a rocky knoll, a sculpture by Aristide Maillol rises out of a sea of blooming hostas. A Japanese spirit walk, whose winding route was thought to ward off evil spirits, floats above a field of iris; outcroppings of bamboo and ostrich ferns mingle with native forest.

A SENSE OF PLACE Historic French estates inspire a California couple to create a dream home of their own, brimming with simple beauty.

Paul Wiseman's client had an explicit vision: She and her husband were building a house in Northern California, and she wanted it to look like a sumptuous French château. On their first meeting with the San Francisco–based interior designer, she handed him a stack of images. "Most of them were of Louis XVI houses in the South of France, but she also wanted a home with modern livability," says Wiseman, who understood the combination perfectly. He happens to be fluent in an improbable range of styles, designing everything from period French, English, and Italian architecture to contemporary interiors with confidence and ease. In this case, he worked with designer Brenda Mickel, architects from the Pacific Peninsula Group, and the landscape designer Thomas Klope to meld the stately French look of the client's tearsheets with a refined modern touch, both indoors and out. "When you have objects from different times," he says, "it keeps the soul of a house going."

Opposite page: The gentle splash of the backyard fountain is audible indoors.

This page: The house's facade and roofline were inspired by 18th-centry French estates.
Opposite page: A lion's head fountain animates the garden.

PURE BEAUTY A resplendent Connecticut garden balances formal architecture with an abundance of blossoms.

A gardener who can cite the Latin names of all 140 varieties of roses in her flowering beds will invariably bring a sense of precision to bear on her cultivated plots. In bucolic Litchfield County, Connecticut, philanthropist Anne Bass has done just that, creating a veritable Eden of color and fragrance that is artfully framed by architectural clipped hedges and generous swaths of lush green with the help of landscape designers Madison Cox and Dan Kiley. The approach has a somewhat counterintuitive effect, emphasizing the romance of blowsy pale roses and blossom-wreathed pergolas so that even at the height of the season, an elegant calm prevails. Sumptuousness never felt so pure and natural.

Opposite page: A grape arbor runs through the estate's cutting garden.

This page: Roses blanket a silo, with blooms below ranging from deep purple to soft cream. Roses and clematis climb an arbor abutting the rose garden. *Opposite page:* A grassy walkway is bordered by Redouté roses and boxwood. *Following pages:* In a part of the garden overlooking the rolling hills of the Litchfield County countryside, an English cider press was repurposed as a pond.

EXOTIC INFLUENCES East meets West in a new Dallas home imbued with an international style and sensibility.

When it comes to mothers-in-law, there are pop songs, T-shirts, and endless jokes attesting to the pitfalls of one of life's most precarious relationships. But Elisa Summers would beg to differ. When she married her husband 17 years ago, she acquired not only a genial spouse but also a charming mother-in-law: Emily Summers, the renowned interior designer with a blue-chip clientele and offices in Dallas and Manhattan.

When Elisa and her husband embarked on building their forever house in Dallas's Highland Park, they hoped to conjure the beauty and ease of a vacation home and gravitated toward an architectural style more often seen in Florida and California than in Texas: Spanish Colonial Revival. Early in the process, Elisa became entranced with a book depicting La Mamounia, the fabled Marrakech palace hotel. The images were an important reference in the design of the house, which was created in conjunction with the esteemed California architect Marc Appleton of Appleton Partners LLP.

Then a year before its completion, Emily traveled with the couple to Morocco and Spain to shop for tiles, doors, pierced-metal lanterns, plaster sconces, and antiques. "We had so much fun exploring the bazaars," Emily says. Clearly, there are benefits to having a mother-in-law who is squarely in your corner.

Opposite page: The entry courtyard's fireplace offers an intimate place to gather in the evenings.

This page: The front gate has a Moroccan motif. *Opposite page:* Rattan furniture and tole palm trees add tropical allure to a loggia.

This page: Cheery potted blooms and climbing vines enliven a walkway. *Opposite page:* A tiled sitting room opens onto the loggia. Pierced-metal lanterns that line the steps to the loggia were found on trips to Morocco and Spain.

Exotic Moroccan details, modern furnishings, and classic Spanish Colonial Revival architecture are blended to create a home that is undeniably original and one of a kind.

TEXAS TRIUMPH *Boxwood hedges, impatiens, and olive trees line a courtyard to create a welcoming scene at a majestic house in Houston, which delicately balances the principles of classic design with a gracious sense of intimacy.*

Opposite page: Built from scratch in Houston's tony River Oaks neighborhood, the home was a highly detailed undertaking—a light-footed dance between French and Italian styles—overseen by decorator J. Randall Powers, architect Drew S. Wommack, and landscape designer Johnny Steele.

PARTY READY A master of exquisite outdoor living spaces cultivates an enduring retreat.

For exterior designer Scott Shrader, creating real outdoor living spaces is about more than what meets the eye: Certain creature comforts have to be provided for the spaces to be truly successful. "If you don't plan on people being warm or cool, or hydrated and fed, they're going back in the house," he says matter-of-factly. That's why Shrader treats the outdoors like the interior rooms of a house. In his world, a tree canopy is the equivalent of a ceiling; if none is available, a trellis can do double duty (with the added bonus of heat lamps unobtrusively integrated for chilly nights). On this four-acre site in Malibu, California, he divided distinct areas for dining, lounging, and cooking. Each has a sense of intimacy and privacy but is still visually connected to the other spaces. The low-key finishes and textures of the outdoor furniture echo the understated gray-and-green palette of the plantings, which Shrader established 15 years ago. And though he has evolved the garden through three different homeowners and some 60 seasons, one thing remains constant: "I never purchase a chair without testing it first," he says. "I'm one for complete comfort."

73

Opposite page: Woven lounge chairs are set against a backdrop of *Agave americana* on a pool deck made of reclaimed scaffolding.

"If you don't plan on people being warm or cool, or hydrated and fed, they're going back in the house," Shrader says matter-of-factly.

This page: Lounge chairs and built-in seating surround a fire pit for a variety of cozy seating options. *Opposite page:* Del Rio gravel anchors the garden, including the dining area. An outdoor kitchen is a lively gathering spot.

PERSONAL SCRAPBOOK A Long Island getaway transforms into a visual tour de force that serves as an incubator for new ideas.

It happens every Friday night. In frenetic Manhattan, after a wild week of running their respective design firms, two men pack a vehicle with bags of drawings, samples, notes, and necessities, plus cats and dogs (two of each), and begin the journey due east. Just one hour and 20 minutes later, as they pull into the village of Bellport, New York, where the streets are lined with picket fences and clapboard cottages, they haven't just switched towns—they've changed their lives.

Designer Dan Fink calls it "moving day," his weekly migration to the former seaport on Long Island's South Shore. Waiting for him there are two elegant structures: a shingled 1833 schoolhouse turned residence and, barely 40 feet away across a narrow lane, a shingle-and-brick building designed by his husband, designer Thomas O'Brien. The latter structure looks straight out of the 1800s—though its addition evokes the 1920s—but the whole composition is a sleight of hand, one in which O'Brien takes great pride. "When we were building it," says O'Brien, "so many people thought it was a house we were renovating. But in fact, it's all new."

The landscape, too, has a sense of timelessness. Crushed gravel paths and a brick allée, lined with wildly abundant plantings, lead to a sunken garden and greenhouse on the property. Fink and O'Brien collaborated with horticulturist Suvi Asch to shape the landscape into a creative laboratory of foliage—firmly rooted in the past, yet forward-thinking and fresh.

Opposite page: Potted annuals and a fig tree flank the entrance to the walled garden.

"There's so much about today that doesn't have character," O'Brien says. "But this place is about time, current and past."

This page: Horticulturist Suvi Asch planted honey locust trees in the allée by the library. *Opposite page:* A Macoun apple tree stands in the walled garden. The sunken garden surrounding the greenhouse is a riot of blooms.

PAST PERFECT In an 18th-century New England farmhouse, a creative couple crafts an inviting, unbuttoned home that seamlessly bridges old and new.

Today, a hornbeam hedge encloses the front garden of this cottage, planted with a double border of perennials, while yews line an allée underplanted with tousled meadow grasses and alliums. But the landscape and the original farmhouse itself are testament to one couple's ability to find charm in patina and imperfections.

Built in the late 18th century, the home was compact, efficient, and beautifully crafted, but also claustrophobically low-ceilinged and startlingly close to the road by modern standards. (It also backed onto a decline so steep that Kahlil Hamady, the architect the owners hired to update it, refers to it as a "cliff"—one that descends into wetlands. "The property defies nearly every building code and zoning law that exists," says Hamady.) Though friends suggested that the couple tear the place down and start all over again, the pair adored the old house and couldn't bear to replace it with the run-of-the-mill mansion. "We wanted to preserve what we had," says the wife.

Equally important was rethinking the landscape so it would interact more felicitously with the expanded house. For this, the couple turned to landscape designer Kathryn Herman of Doyle Herman Design Associates, who terraced the hillside, planted an orchard and the allée, and constructed outdoor rooms at every level to draw people into the garden. It's not all prim hedges: thyme, lavender, and an antique climbing rose are planted in the joints of old stone steps, and an assortment of fruit trees grows among fescue grasses mowed in a diamond pattern. "There's a dynamic interaction," she says, "between formality and something a little wild."

81

Opposite page: Yews, meadow grasses, and alliums border a grassy walkway. *Following pages:* Fruit trees grow among fescue grasses.

"There's a dynamic interaction between formality and something a little wild," says landscape designer Kathryn Herman.

85

This page: Antique roses grow along a stone wall. *Opposite page:* A hornbeam hedge encircles the front garden, planted with a double border of perennials. Thyme, lavender, and an antique climbing rose grow from the joints of the stone steps for a timeworn look.

PARADISE FOUND An oceanfront estate's alfresco spaces are fashioned with quiet grace and glamour.

After designer David Kleinberg's longtime clients decided to sell their beloved Palm Beach house—an offer out of the blue had been too good to refuse—they sought a new home, this time on the ocean, as they had long fancied. Flying down to inspect it, Kleinberg found a Spanish Colonial–style house with a classic and well-conceived floor plan of graciously proportioned rooms by the award-winning Kirchhoff and Associates Architects that blissfully welcomed the outdoors. A lush landscape devised by the equally illustrious Keith Williams & Mario Nievera of Nievera Williams Landscape Architecture made for a complete, artful masterpiece. Lance Scott, a partner at David Kleinberg Design Associates, masterminded an ultrachic respite inside, as well as perfect perches for languorous living on the home's luxurious outdoor loggias, which round out its tropical allure and island glamour.

Opposite page: A breezy, oceanfront loggia is the setting for long, leisurely lunches. *Following pages:* The interior courtyard is a sheltered oasis filled with manicured greenery, lush bougainvillea, and a pool for respite on hot days.

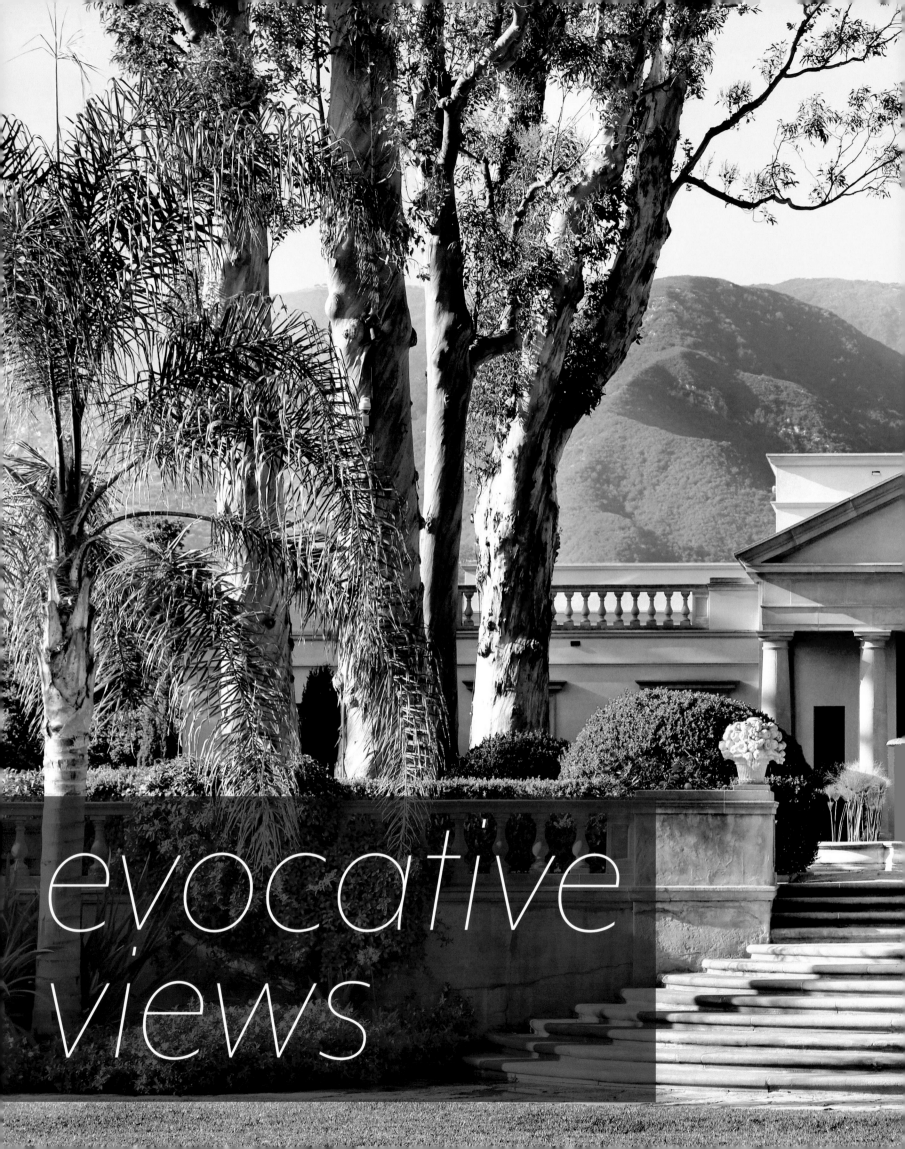

evocative
views

There's an inevitable moment of wonder as a tantalizing vista unfolds—a gasp, a sigh. Perched atop hillsides, tucked into mountain ranges, or deftly nestled where land meets the sea, these homes are rich with sweeping panoramas and revel in that moment of discovery.

Preceding pages: The stately residence features a Palladian-style portico designed by Santa Barbara architect Jack Lionel Warner. *Opposite page:* Views of the Santa Ynez Mountains lie beyond the terrace.

PEACEFUL KINGDOM For a Louisiana couple looking for a second home on the West Coast, an estate with a gracious spirit offers a sense of serenity and splendor nestled amid the rolling hills of Santa Barbara.

"When we drove onto the property for the first time, a sense of peace came over me," says the wife, who, with her husband, bought the Montecito, California, residence as a second home. Native Louisianans, the family wanted a place to spend summers with their West Coast–based children and friends. Enthralled with the Santa Barbara enclave's stunning natural beauty, she was drawn to both the house, set among eucalyptus and oak, and its history. She turned to her friend, designer Ann Holden, who shared her reverence for the past and transformed the property into a home for a thoroughly modern family with a gentle hand.

In its belle époque prime, the aptly named Arcady was the 148-acre estate of industrialist George Owen Knapp. Host to dignitaries, socialites, and numerous soirees, Arcady was elaborately developed and celebrated for its heart-stopping views, storied gardens, and unusual outbuildings. But as times and fortunes changed, the estate was eventually subdivided in the 1940s; the couple's stately home, its gracious aura still intact, was initially conceived as a music pavilion and underground ballroom. When it was built, only the pavilion's staircase, terrace, and fountain were visible from the approach. Its ballroom and sunken gardens were tantalizingly out of view. In the 1950s, a residence was constructed atop the terrace, and the classical Palladian-style portico was added in the early 2000s. Imposing and yet entirely appropriate in setting and scale, the architecture achieves the kind of visual harmony that imparts a sense of order and calm. The glamorous pool, also a 1950s addition, is made all the more romantic with its halo of oleander and cypress. The verdant gardens—brimming with fountains, lush plantings, and ideal spots for outdoor entertaining—remain as magical as ever.

Opposite page: The Mediterranean-inspired pool and fountain are flanked by blooming oleander and cypress trees.

GRACE NOTES Weathered materials and ethereal hues lend a new beach house an old soul.

Beautiful old architectural elements can be presented in a clean, modern way. They can speak of the past, but without the ponderousness. They can even be recast as lighthearted players in a fresh new drama that's all about la dolce vita, American style. Or so goes the thinking behind a new, French Provincial–inspired California beach house planted in the sands of Orange County and decorated by Ohara Davies-Gaetano. Its owners wanted a magical place to unwind in style, but one thing was certain—they didn't want the house to scream its newness. Instead, they got depth and a good whiff of the past, indoors and out. Elegant and understated, the great room opens onto a loggia perched over the surf, all enveloped in an ethereal matte softness. "It's like a foggy morning," Davies-Gaetano observes. "But when the sun is shining brightly, the whole house comes to life."

Opposite page: A French limestone door surround sets a stately mood. *Following pages:* Retractable steel doors open the great room to Pacific Ocean views.

RETURN TO EDEN On a promontory overlooking the Tyrrhenian Sea, one of Italy's reigning families of design escapes to their lush island paradise.

On Lipari, one of the eight Aeolian Islands that appear to have been kicked into the Mediterranean by the toe of Italy's boot, is an idyll perched on a hill. With almost as many terraces (three) as bedrooms (four), and with gardens nearly three times the size of the 2,100-square-foot house, Casa di Pino is clearly designed for doing most of one's living outside. The property's name—which translates to "pine-tree house"—alludes to the ridge of conifers that surround the property. Those trees are an anomaly in the area, but the olive, citrus, fig, and palm trees, plus cacti and prickly pears, that ring the house are not. Nor is the terraced vegetable garden, where the acidic volcanic soil, amassed from half a million years of eruptions that formed the islands, produces superior vegetables. (The couple makes their own olive oil from the trees on the property and pick grapes from the arbor for eating out of hand.) "We spend all of the summer in the outdoor living room just off the kitchen," says the wife. At the villa, the couple largely dine alfresco, with a breathtaking view to the endless sea. Even the swimming pool is sited for maximum views of the neighboring islands rising up out of the deep blue water in the distance.

III

Opposite page: Outdoor entertaining is second nature at Casa di Pino. *Following pages:* The swimming pool overlooks the Aeolian Islands.

In the distance, the islands of Salina, Filicudi, and Alicudi—where electricity arrived in 1950 and donkeys are the latest method of transport—rise up out of the deep blue water.

This page: A chaise amid the palms offers afternoon respite. *Opposite page:* A stripe of Sicilian tiles enlivens a terrace's cement floor.

A GRAND PLAN Among groves of olive trees and Italian cypress, a newly built estate in Montecito merges the fantasy of Mediterranean living with sun-kissed California style.

It all began with two yards of mossy green Fortuny fabric, purchased in a tiny antique-fabric shop in Venice more than 20 yers ago and stored away on the shelf of a bookcase. "We came to Richard," says the client, referring to the quintessentially Californian designer Richard Hallberg, "I told him that I love Italy, that Venice is my favorite city. I took out the fabric and said, 'This is where we should start.'"

And in a way, that piece of fabric—at least the airy, fine feel of it—is where it ended, too. The 8,000-square-foot house, on three acres in Montecito, California, embodies the lush elegance of a European villa burnished with contemporary West Coast charm. The site, with magnificent views, had for two decades held the couple's lovely, modern Mediterranean-style house, but they knew they wouldn't be happy until it was replaced with a residence that reminded them more of the sunbaked Tuscany of their dreams and countless visits. So Hallberg worked with the arcitectural firm Appleton Partners LLP and landscape design firm Clark & White to fashion an environment in which every element is hand-honed—from stone to wood to plaster and gilding—lending a patina of gracious tradition. Symmetry, another Hallberg hallmark, was a priority for the home-owners. The entrance, grand yet simple, is flanked by olive trees; the loggia, where the couple frequently have dinner parties, is a geometric harmony of arches and straight lines. Throughout the outdoor spaces, the colors are calming and neutral, with shots of that gentle green inspired by the Fortuny fabric.

Opposite page: Cypress and olive trees recall a Tuscan villa.

This page: Curtains and slipcovered chairs give an open-air dining space indoor comfort. *Opposite page:* For Hallberg, the blank canvas of new construction is invigorating; the resulting Tuscan-inspired villa's entry is a study in modernized references, timeworn materials, and symmetry.

INDEPENDENT SPIRIT With her photographer's eye, an artist imbues her riverside Victorian with global influences from her far-flung travels.

"It's one of the most gorgeous places in the world," says fine-art photographer Kate Cordsen of the bluff overlooking the Connecticut River where she lives. The river's otherworldly light and the tiny New England village it hugs drew the artist and her husband there decades ago; the handsome Italianate Victorian they share with their teenage children is what kept them rooted to the place. Though built in 1981 on a lot that once housed one of New England's major shipbuilders, the four-bedroom house looks as though it has proudly stood there for more than a century. "The couple who built it lovingly patched together a handful of salvaged Victorian houses to make a whole," Cordsen explains. Which is exactly how she likes it: "In my work, and in life, for that matter, I appreciate seeing the hand of the artist, an adventurous spirit, combining old and new, and embracing imperfection."

Opposite page: After buying the property, Cordsen brightened the walls, restored the mahogany trim along with the oak and walnut floors, and opened up the rooms to make the most of the reflected light off the river— which guests enjoy over meals on the porch.

This page: The majesty of the Italianate Victorian belies the fact that it was built in the 1980s, with a lush garden created by River-End Landscaping *Opposite page:* The porch serves as a welcoming outdoor living room for alfresco entertaining.

STAR QUALITY An iconic Atlanta home with a classic pedigree is now filled with a youthful exuberance reflective of the family that calls it home.

Two years ago, a young Atlanta couple embarked on the thrill ride of renovation when they purchased a 1934 Regency-style house and set out to update it while preserving its remarkably intact original features: doors, moldings, fireplaces, wood floors, and even single-pane windows that still open via pulleys and weighted ropes. The home's original architect surely would have approved: Georgia native Philip Shutze studied architecture at Columbia University in New York and the American Academy in Rome, then returned to author many fine classical-style homes and buildings around Atlanta in the 1920s and 30s.

The couple called Atlanta-based interior designer Melanie Turner—who had not only designed two previous residences for them but also lives in a Shutze house herself—to transform the home by way of tiger-print velvet, pale pink walls, and deep lavender accents galore. Turner worked with local architect Yong Pak on a section of the home that had been added a few years earlier ("It was a big vanilla box, so we layered in a lot of details," Turner says) and the long list of upgrades, including a new kitchen, a pool pavilion, and terraces. Today, the house is alive with color—a vibrant setting for an amiable family of five, plus a pair of prancing cockapoos. Nothing is precious here—and the couple wouldn't have it any other way. "Everything can be touched and felt and sat on and slept in," says the wife. "And that's what we really love."

125

Opposite page: Framed by a verdant garden designed by Land Plus Associates, the pool pavilion is an elegant setting for outdoor soirees. *Following pages:* Despite the glamorous formality of the design, the property is imbued with the youth and energy of the homeowners—a stunning playground for their young family.

PERFECTLY SUITED After landing her dream house in a twist of fate, tastemaker Tara Shaw revels in the Haussmann-inspired property's easy grace.

When her house in New Orleans was being built—for someone else—designer Tara Shaw walked by it every day. "I thought, 'This can't be New Orleans,'" she says. She loved its "severe front," reminiscent of the Haussmann facades in Paris, and a wall around the property that "seemed to hide a secret courtyard." Although she lived in a charming Victorian at the time, it was French architecture she adored. The homeowner was a Francophile, too, and had asked local architect Barry Fox to design a house modeled after one he'd seen in France.

As Shaw watched the progress, she thought she might like to tackle a similar project one day. "I never thought this one would come on the market," she says. When it did, she had to buy it: "It was as though it were built for me." Shaw turned to landscape designer Byron Adams to create formal gardens that mirror the stately facade. She blanketed the interior of the home in shades of white, but the exterior is adorned in a medley of neatly clipped green—her own secret garden.

129

Oppositepage: Formal hedges flank the entrance to the house. *Following pages:* The flagstone pool surround complements the graceful curves of the terrace.

SUNSHINE STATE A Mediterranean Revival home in Florida combines classicism with a nod to the new.

Lou Marotta's move from New York to Florida was the realization of a dream deferred—the antiques dealer and interior designer was waiting for his husband, lawyer Michael Fullwood, to retire. Though the couple had originally envisioned a move to Palm Beach, the siren of a 1926 Mediterranean Revival drew them across the bridge to the El Cid Historic District in West Palm Beach, whose laid-back vibe was immensely appealing. "We wanted a warm, casual setting where we could entertain in a relaxed way," Marotta explains. "Moorish architecture is all about fantasy, so the house and the neighborhood suited us perfectly."

Outside, the house is enveloped in Marotta's sublime gardens, which give him a great deal of pleasure but have also proven to be a challenge for this avid horticulturist. "I now know that plants in this part of Florida are dormant all winter," he says. "The leaves are green, but nothing actually blooms until June." Not wanting to wait, he augments his plantings with pots of flowering succulents, hibiscus, begonias, and lantanas, as well as orchids, which hang from an almighty gumbo-limbo tree at the home's entrance. A pebbled walkway is lined with creeping fig that Marotta trained into a new low hedge and jazzed up with hot-pink bromeliads.

On the other side of the property, which faces Lake Worth Lagoon, another garden boasts purple Mexican petunias and *podocarpus* clipped into topiary balls. A sculptural agave plant marks the place where drinks are served at sunset. Unsurprisingly, dinner at the couple's house—which as been given the moniker Casa de Perro ("House of the Dog") in honor of their Scottish deerhound—is a coveted invitation in this part of Florida. All of a sudden, everyone wants to be in the doghouse.

133

This page: A spray of orchids is an elegant focal point on a terra-cotta-studded terrace.

"We wanted a warm, casual setting where we could entertain in a relaxed way," Marotta explains. "Moorish architecture is all about fantasy, so the house and the neighborhood suited us perfectly."

135

This page: The home's leafy entrance and a series of stepping stones into the garden are equally enchanting.
Opposite page: A pair of antique French carved-stone figures depicting Greek philosophers overlooks the swimming pool, while moveable chaises offer casual seating.

This page: Terra-cotta tiles set into the terrace in a windowpane pattern ground the restful outdoor seating area. *Opposite page:* A carved 1930s Italian dining table holds court on the terrace, which faces Lake Worth Lagoon.

AMERICAN REVIVAL *A stately Colonial-style home in Connecticut features a series of intimate outdoor rooms that are as thoughtfully curated as the residence's interior spaces. Even art was considered: a contemporary poolside sculpture adds a dramatic, unexpected focal point to the timeless surroundings.*

This page: The Ferguson & Shamamian Architects-designed home is beautifully enveloped in a landscape deftly crafted by Doyle Herman Design Associates.

This page: Clipped boxwoods add an undulating texture to the garden. *Following pages:* Willa, a Labrador retriever, lounges beside the pool.

PACIFIC PARADISE At a ranch high in the mountains above Malibu, a veritable fantasyland perches among the clouds.

"I have exactly one pair of pants," say Hutton Wilkinson. The California designer—whose jewelry and interiors exude maximalist panache—hasn't fallen on hard times. Rather, he is taking inventory of the uncharacteristically minimalist wardrobe he stocks at Argyle Farm, his 100-acre mountaintop retreat in Malibu. "A couple of shirts, some tennis clothes, and shoes," he lists. "And swim trunks. That's it. Very easy and thoughtless."

Glorious abandon is, indeed, the point of this idyll overlooking the Pacific, a getaway that serves as an antidote to the glittery life he and his wife, Ruth, lead in Beverly Hills. In town, they preside over a three-story palazzo filled with Venetian paintings and leopard-print carpets—a house that's a frequent setting for themed parties. "You are served drinks, and you dress up," Wilkinson says. By contrast, "at the farm in Malibu, you get your own drinks—and you can wear whatever you like."

At the center of the farm is an Adirondack-style lodge that the couple purchased some two decades ago. Built in the late 1940s of stone and rough-sawn lumber, the main house sits surrounded by meandering walkways, a vegetable garden, a tennis court, a sparkling pool, and all manner of architectural follies, including a wiry coral pagoda made from a vintage elevator cage that once whisked guests up and down in the Hollywood Hotel. A big night at the lodge—where there is no cell-phone reception or Internet—doesn't mean galas and gowns; it means literally gazing at "every star and constellation in the universe," Wilkinson says. "And when it's cold and overcast at the beach, we retreat above the clouds."

145

Opposite page: A coral pagoda fashioned from a vintage elevator cage is one of the property's many follies.

This page: Lush tropical foliage leads up the steps to the pool. *Opposite page:* Alfresco entertaining is a favorite pastime. *Following pages:* A bust of Julius Caesar is a tribute to the late designer Tony Duquette, who was a friend and business partner, and whose ranch was nearby.

CALIFORNIA COOL French Country style inspires an idyllic retreat.

Grandeur need not be measured in square feet and ornate details. "There's a certain nobility in simplicity," says Greg Stewart, principal at Orlando Diaz-Azcuy Design Associates (ODADA), of a pared-down French Country–style home on 24 acres in Carmel Valley, California, bordered by an inspiring mountain view. The house was an encore for the San Francisco design firm, which had previously worked with the architect, the late Andrew Batey, on a residence in Napa. "Andrew knew how to translate the materials and attitudes of a traditional building into the kind of home people want to live in today," recalls legendary designer Orlando Diaz-Azcuy of his collaborator.

Built on a parcel of land that was once part of a large preserve the homeowners loved to hike through, the resulting home is a contemporary version of French neoclassical design, at once streamlined and stately. "The inspiration came from the work of Louis XIV's military engineer, who modernized all the forts in the country," Stewart explains. Set into the base of a rolling hillside, the curved, windowless facade of the house has the austere appearance of a garrison.

Stewart enlivened the mostly neutral palette inside with accents from the panoramic views: gold from the native grasses, the green of the leaves on the backyard's ancient oak, and the deep teal of the surrounding Big Sur region. "In this setting, the simpler and more natural, the better," he said.

151

Opposite page: The limestone flooring extends to the terrace for a seamless indoor-outdoor transition.
Following pages: The home's architecture maximizes the beauty of the area's surrounding landscape.

SIMPLY SERENE Overlooking the white-as-sugar beaches and azure waters of the Gulf of Mexico, a sun-drenched Florida residence proves that less is indeed more.

At first sight, Alys Beach comes as a surprise to travelers meandering down the Gulf coast's busy Highway 30A. It's the site of a gleaming oasis where Nashville designer Rozanne Jackson collaborated with husband-and-wife architectural team Marieanne Khoury-Vogt and Erik Vogt, the stylistic godparents of the town's jasmine-draped streets since the area's founding in 2003, on a second home for a Tennessee family. The house is inspired by the simple design vocabulary of Bermuda and the exuberant parapets and crenellations of North Africa. "The architecture feels familiar, but you can't pinpoint it," says Vogt.

Gleaming white villas, walled gardens, and sparkling fountains—all set off by a cerulean sea—feel more Moroccan than down-home Florida Panhandle. A second-floor living room extends the full width of the house for 180-degree vistas, and a porch with forever views juts from the room like a captain's bridge. But the home's anchor is set firmly ashore: The ground-level pool and outdoor dining area nestle down deep into dunes that are covered in a thick mantle of beach scrub, such that only the gentle murmur of the waves and the occasional nesting sea turtle let you know that the Gulf is very near.

155

Opposite page: Slipcovered swivel chairs are perfectly positioned for admiring the oceanfront sunsets.

"This house is so outside of anyone's expectations," says designer Rozanne Jackson. "It's always the same reaction: 'Wow! Where am I?'"

This page: The living room boasts two 10-foot-long sofas—and 180-degree ocean views. *Opposite page:* The cypress shutters, copper eaves, and limestone accents of this stucco villa were chosen to age gracefully. Cast concrete spheres lure visitors down the walkway to a fountain.

This page: A stucco arch gracefully frames the outdoor dining room. *Opposite page:* The property includes a sheltered pool.

romantic
retreats

Summertime is ripe with simple pleasures, like the feeling of walking barefoot through the grass or dipping toes into the glimmering pool. These sun-kissed spaces capture that sense of laid-back luxury with easy elegance and gracious charm.

OUT EAST On the weekends, two New York City creatives trade city life for sun, fun, and relaxation at their 19th-century Hamptons home.

Most people in search of a house insist its ceilings be intact, but for one couple, even an ominously sagging roofline couldn't dissuade them. The first thing the pair noticed on their initial visit to the 1885 Shingle-style farmhouse they now call their home away from home was the water pouring through the shingles on the second floor. It was a sign of things to come. "The place was so charming, even though the living room was flooded and the ceiling was about four feet from the floor," says one. They tore the place back to the studs and built it up again, tweaking the first floor layout for informal entertaining. In the winter, they eat and play Scrabble around the living room fireplace; in the summer, friends gather outside to grill, swim, hang out on the trellised back deck—and join heated games of pétanque on the gravel court that the couple added to the driveway. "I always let him say he wins," says the other. "But the truth is, I beat him every time."

Opposite page: When the couple moved in, the Rosco farmhouse—as it's known locally in honor of the original family who built it—was an important Southampton landmark in need of preservation; today, the beach vibes start with the surfboard that hangs over the back door.

This page: The homeowners enjoy an unfussy, informal approach to outdoor entertaining. *Opposite page:* Cobalt accents—from throw pillows and chaises to the tiles that line the pool—add a convivial note to the landscape.

The couple is the exception to
the renovation-as-relationship-
wrecker rule; they met 20 years
and 4 houses ago. Not even
this gut renovation threw them.
They tore the place down to the
studs and built it back up again.

ROOM TO ROAM
The simple charms of rural life—fresh air, more space, and a slower pace—inspired a magical oasis in the rolling hills of Ojai.

Brooke and Steve Giannetti's Patina Farm in the small-town, artsy enclave of Ojai, California, is a story of choices, in design and in life. The husband-and-wife team—he's an architect, she's a decorator—made the decision to leave the bustle of Los Angeles for a more rural setting. Though they did manage a small flock of chickens in their charming Santa Monica home, their menagerie has now expanded to include dogs, miniature donkeys, goats, and a rabbit.

On four and a half acres of undulant meadow and pasture, designed in collaboration with landscape designer Margaret Grace, the house nestles among cypress and oak, roses and lavender, boxwood gardens, meandering native plantings, and stone terraces that all look as if they've been tended through generations rather than started from scratch in 2012. Indeed, says Steve, first-time visitors invariably ask what was original and what was added on. "To make it look natural, you have to leave it natural," he says. "We named it Patina Farm for a reason," adds Brooke. "It's the idea that you use natural materials and let them age gracefully over time—I'm trying to do that myself, too."

Opposite page: The entrance to Patina Farm frames picture-perfect views of the landscape beyond.

This page: A profusion of white roses and lavender perfumes the landscape around the house. *Opposite page:* The luxurious glassed-in master bath offers the best of both indoor and outdoor bathing.

This page: Large-scale glass doors on both sides of the dining room blur the line between indoors and out.
Opposite page: Informal meals unfold in the shade of a majestic tree next to a cluster of clipped shrubs and an antique fountain that looks as though its been there for generations.

This page: Evenings unfold on the corner banquette that anchors the fireplace. *Opposite page:* Hens gather in the kitchen garden. A collection of vintage watering cans and flower pots decorates the chicken coop.

The rambling nature of the property gives it a sense of timelessness. Each part of the house and outbuildings called for materials consistent with its unique character: from stucco and terra-cotta to barn siding and corrugated metal.

175

SUMMER SPLENDOR A run-of-the-mill South Florida ranch house perched on the coast is stunningly reborn as a chic, sun-drenched family retreat celebrating island style and gracious outdoor living.

A serpentine gravel drive bordered by palms and sea grapes curves to reveal a refined white-stucco compound whose cool, streamlined simplicity belies the grandeur that unfolds inside. Beyond the louvered front door, a loggia supplants the traditional entry hall—a long passageway that connects the main house, the pool house, and the guesthouse, all anchored around a lush central courtyard.

The property was not always so inspired. When the homeowners purchased the rambling 1970s ranch, they had reconstruction, not renovation, in mind. "It had some interesting spaces inside, but there wasn't much about it that we wanted to keep," says D. Stanley Dixon, the mastermind behind the beachfront property's redesign. But before work began, the family spent a season in the house and came to admire some of its uniquely "old Florida" details—the meandering one-story floor plan, terrazzo floors, and cypress walls. In the end, they opted for an expansive face-lift that retained some of the charms of the house they had fallen in love with.

Dixon was influenced by the exuberant architecture of warm-weather locales like Bermuda, Morocco, and Greece. "My vision was to take these worldly styles and blend them together," he says. He added an evocative stepped roof with graphic scalloped gable ends and built-in niches to the facade; other details, like Chippendale fretwork screens in windows flanking the front door, are inspired by British Colonial architecture.

Intimate outdoor rooms are family-friendly without losing their elegance. Pristine terraces close to the house ease seamlessly into loose, less structured gardens where the family's children play. On the loggia, sited to feature breathtaking views of the beach, gurgling fountains compete with the sound of the surf. Every corner is thoughtfully outfitted with a place to unwind and relax—a secluded oasis ideally suited for soaking up the Florida sun.

177

Opposite page: Hand-painted tiles line the outdoor shower; a crush of bougainvillea round the curves of the property's scrollwork details.

This page: The distinctive stepped roof was inspired by the traditional style of a Bermudian buttery, an outdoor larder. *Opposite page:* A sense of serenity prevails thanks to the pared-down palette and finishes, including limewashed cypress accents against chalky-white plaster and custom lanterns fitted with lavender glass to cast a rosy evening glow.

ART OF ARRIVAL   A new house in Dallas expertly merges classical French architecture and lush plantings to create a unique sense of place.

"I wanted to create a magic kingdom, something elegant and glamorous without being pompous," said the late designer Beverly Field of the home she helped create for a Dallas client. Neoclassical limestone pavilions of France, with their clean, restrained symmetry and gracious proportion, were the starting point. Los Angeles architect Richardson Robertson III, known for his classical style, was chosen to design the home and the grounds. Although his client wanted a traditional design, he understood that the house— a stunning cut-limestone design with a stately entrance flanked by an allée—needed to reflect her spirit: "very with it and of-the-moment," he says.

Opposite page: The pleached live oaks that line the driveway of this newly constructed Dallas manse imbue a sense of timelessness.

HAMPTONS HIDEAWAY A Dallas designer brings her pattern-happy approach to a Southampton retreat.

Kelli Ford sought a sense of deliberate calm in her Southampton summer escape, an airy six-bedroom charmer built right on the dunes. The Dallas-based designer worked with architect Peter Pennoyer to rebuild the original house—a beautifully classic shingled cottage with a spacious wraparound porch. The space is more than just about entertaining. "We live on that porch," she says. "It's an extension of the living room." With panoramic views—lush gardens by landscape firm Deborah Nevins & Associates that complement views of placid Shinnecock Bay in front and the vast, salty Atlantic in back—the property evokes a sense of nostalgia and ease. "I put the windows down in the car as we're driving up, because you can smell the ocean, and the privet, and the freshly mowed grass," says Ford. "It transports me, and everyone in my family, to a state of relaxation, happiness, and peace."

Opposite page: Wicker seating outfitted in summery stripes, oversized checks, and a splash of watermelon create a refined but laid-back space. *Following pages:* The pool area is fresh, fun—and luxurious without a hint of pretension.

LONDON CALLING *For a townhouse in Belgravia, Jean-Louis Deniot translates his high-voltage French style into a glamorous family home, complete with an urban outdoor retreat. Paired with the cityscape's classical architecture, the space's contemporary design is a magical, unexpected surprise.*

Opposite page: Sliding doors in the dining room open onto the terrace. "I always used to be out and about, but now I prefer to hang out here," says the homeowner.

SWEET CAROLINA It was love at sight for a couple who stumbled upon their future Low Country home while perusing the morning paper.

In 1859, as Civil War drums began to beat steadily louder, Beaufort, South Carolina, resident Dr. Joseph Johnson made an unlikely decision: He was going to build the largest, most magnificent house in town. And despite a Union blockade of the ship carrying his European balustrades, ironwork, and marble fireplace mantels, he did just that. At a breathtaking 11,000 square feet, with 23 rooms and 79 windows, locals long ago dubbed it "the Castle" for its crenellated parapet and the surrounding salt marsh, which resembles a moat at high tide.

For a couple on a 100-acre farm in Virginia horse country, it is the perfect getaway. They were not in the market for a second home, but the baronial manse caught the husband's eye as he leafed through the *Wall Street Journal*. "He turned the page and said to me, 'Look at this crazy house for sale! Let's go take a look, just for fun.'" They visited—and promptly fell in love with the property. Now, the couple kicks off every summer by cramming the car with dahlias from their Virginia garden and driving nine hours south to host an annual "dahlia party" on the Castle's porch. The intricate jib windows that double as doors from the living room to the porch are flung open. And as evening approaches, the house glows gray to tan to pink as the sun sinks behind a canopy of live oaks that are as majestic as—and hundreds of years older than—the house itself.

Opposite page: A traditional jib window leads to the porch.

This page: The 1861 house was designed as a copy of an English manor. *Opposite page:* The porch ceiling is painted in a soft blue-green hue that's traditionally believed to ward off ghosts.

GEORGIAN REVIVAL *A historic Richmond, Virginia, property—one of 21 homes in the area designed by renowned architect William Lawrence Bottomley in the 1920s and '30s—got a sensitive, supremely elegant renovation for a thoroughly modern family. Even the terrace's Palladian arches retain their original grace.*

Opposite page: The homeowners tapped Richmond architect Madison Spencer to guide them through a renovation that preserved the home's Georgian Revival character.

This page: Landscape design by Rieley & Associates highlights a superb view. *Opposite page:* A Palladian arch on the terrace makes a graphic statement against crisp white walls and furnishings.

CLASSIC CHARM
An orangery filled with the intoxicating scent of citrus is the perfect setting for bringing the delights of the outdoors in.

Even in the relatively temperate climate of Dallas, orange trees are a wintertime godsend—a fragrant harbinger of sun-kissed warmth, however much the wind howls. For a longtime client of Dallas-based interior designer Cathy Kincaid, citrus trees are so cheering and delightful that she decided to commission architect J. Wilson Fuqua to build an orangery next to her home in the city's leafy Highland Park neighborhood.

Historically, the orangery was more than just a cold-weather greenhouse for orange and lemon trees: In fashionable European residences from the 17th to 19th centuries, these conservatories were a lush and aromatic extension of the home. This one in Dallas, with its windowed walls and curved sky-blue ceiling, was designed in the same spirit—inspired by both the 17th-century model on the grounds of Versailles and the Edwin Lutyens—designed version at Hestercombe House in England. Kincaid furnished the interior with a classical scheme, including symmetrical furniture arrangements and antique paintings that frame the sitting area. The palette of neutrals and pale blues conveys an aura of calm. Most of all, the sun-dappled space is designed for entertaining. "It's a dreamy place for luncheons or cocktails before dinner," Kincaid says. And to make watering the trees easy, the periphery of the main room's antique floors were lined with drains—laser-cut bronze grates with very small openings so you can't get a high heel stuck. In other words, it's party-ready.

197

This page: The orangery's classical facade includes French doors that open onto the boxwood-filled landscape designed by Paul Fields.

This page: A sky-blue ceiling lends an ethereal note. *Opposite page:* Natural light and greenery create the feel of a garden indoors.

This page: A stone pathway leads to sculptures and vine-covered structures that nestle into the landscape.
Opposite page: A curving pool is tucked behind a pavilion.

203

This page: A canoe floats at the ready within a stone boathouse. *Opposite page:* From the orangery, stepping stones guide the way down the sloping lawn to the water's edge.

ROMANTIC BY NATURE In a light-filled house in the Hollywood Hills, European elegance meets casual California style for a polished yet relaxed sensibility.

"Los Angeles is a special place because you can live outside all year long," says designer Mark D. Sikes. "We wanted to take full advantage of that." At the Mediterranean-influenced house in the Hollywood Hills that he shares with his partner, every room opens to the garden—windows and French doors flung open to draw in the breeze. "There's not a spot in the house where you can't hear the gurgling fountain," he says. The garden is surrounded by a 12-foot-high ficus hedge, giving the property a sense of intimacy and privacy that seems to keep the world at bay. "It completely takes you away from it all," Sikes says. "You feel like you could be anywhere: Santa Barbara, Italy, the South of France."

Fittingly, the couple forgo the dining room for entertaining, preferring instead to serve dinner in the living room. Guests invariably spill out into the garden, a habit their hosts encourage. "People gravitate to the terrace, and I treat it as an extension of the living room," says Sikes. "I keep some of my blue-and-white porcelain there, and we'll drag out our French upholstered chairs. I cherish this indoor-outdoor lifestyle."

205

Opposite page: A balcony off the master bedroom, shaded by a striped awning, overlooks the garden.

This page: In his living room, Sikes replaced windows with French doors for easy access to the garden. *Opposite page:* Enclosed by ficus, the terraced garden keeps the rest of the world at bay.

EASY BREEZY After selling her longtime Santa Monica home on a whim, a designer finds a Venice, California, bungalow to be the ideal pit stop—and the perfect showcase for her charming prints and casual style.

Kathryn M. Ireland had to find a new home, and quickly. For more than two decades, the British-born decorator had lived in the same 1920s house in Santa Monica, California, where she raised her three sons, now all in their 20s. Inspired by the home's Spanish Colonial Revival architecture, she'd also perfected her personal decorating style inside its stucco walls, one that marries traditional English and romantic Mediterranean looks and tosses in touches of boho and pops of color. Still, she sometimes fantasized about making a change. So when a real estate agent approached her in April 2015 with a "really great" unsolicited offer, the designer said yes—a bit hastily, she now admits. "I got seller's remorse," says Ireland, especially when her kids—one of whom was still at home—learned of her decision. "I pulled the rug out from under them," she says. Over the course of two days, she scoured open houses for a new nest for her brood. One of them was a newly built white-clapboard cottage in the nearby hip enclave of Venice. The 2,700-square-foot home had high ceilings, French doors, and a leafy backyard with ample space for entertaining. "The bones were really good," she says. "It was so nice to be able to just move in and decorate."

Ireland's breezy style translates to equally unfussy outdoor entertaining—although she always has an abundance of linens on hand, she admits to often improvising the rest. Beyond the perfection of her tossed-together tablescapes, there's another serious upside to Ireland's relaxed approach: There's always room for one more at the table.

209

Opposite page: Inspired by the beachy feel of the neighborhood, Ireland embraced a color palette of bright, summery blues. *Following pages:* Spherical wicker lights dance in the breeze over the outdoor dining table. A round table in the garden is perfect for breakfast for two. Guests gather around the fire pit in the evenings.

Beyond the perfection of her
tossed-together tablescapes,
there's another serious upside
to Ireland's relaxed approach:
Extra guests are always
welcome.

GRAND TRADITIONS *After a top-to-bottom renovation, a Shingle-style house on Long Island proves that comfort doesn't have to be sacrificed for style. Designer David Kleinberg chose a neutral palette punctuated by pale blues that is perfectly in sync with the views of the water. "Sometimes we gravitate to obvious color choices because they are the right choices," he says.*

Opposite page: The porch is a timeless, tranquil retreat.

This page: The manicured pool area, designed by architect and landscape designer Kevin Murphy, is bordered by the sea and lush old-growth trees.

HIGH IMPACT With a client open to bold ideas, designer Nick Olsen takes a no-holds-barred approach to color and pattern.

For a 36-year-old Manhattan real-estate broker, the four-bedroom Colonial-era cottage in Dutchess County, New York, was a cozy winter-weekend escape. "It was a bit mumsy when it was on the market, but the location, property, provenance, and architectural significance of the house drew me straight to it," says the homeowner.

Built in 1747, the unassuming clapboard homestead is purported to have once housed a captain in the War of 1812—a detail the homeowner loves about the place, as much as he cherishes the rolling hills, pond, and barn that make up the property. With so much to recommend it, he was not fazed by the dowdy design. That's because the affable bachelor had a secret weapon in interior designer Nick Olsen, who is known for turning color into epic gesture. "He wanted a fantasy hunting lodge—lots of plaid and tartan," says the designer, who also transformed the outdoor entertaining areas with an eclectic mix of furnishings that would feel right at home indoors. But in Olsen's hands, the cottage conjures the sartorial spirit of its owner more than that of Teddy Roosevelt or Ernest Hemingway. "Nick understood what I wanted better than I did," says the homeowner.

217

Opposite page: The porch ceiling, painted in a pale sky blue, recalls sunny days.

This page: The clapboard house was built in 1747. *Opposite page:* Olsen mixed a modern table with rustic chairs for a refreshing dining scene on the front porch.

A BOUNTY OF BLOOMS At her Nantucket home, artist Cathy Graham hosts fun and festive gatherings with flowers from the garden and gifts from the heart.

Flowers don't hold back—bursting forth from buds each spring, even in the most daunting of circumstances—and neither does illustrator and floral maestro Cathy Graham, especially when entertaining. In any season, her tablescapes are as lush as sumptuous peonies, dotted with anything from foxgloves and clematis to miniature dollhouse furniture in equal abundance. "If I have an elegant flower arrangement, I can get away with adding something completely ridiculous," says Graham, who hosts frequent parties at her Manhattan townhouse and Nantucket retreat. Her flowers and tablesettings are loosely inspired by Constance Spry, the British florist famous for high-profile events (the queen's coronation) and innovation (she was purportedly the first florist to add kale to an arrangement). Graham, too, is a boundary pusher, dotting the table with whimsical antiques or dangling crystal chandelier pieces from the ceiling with fishing wire so they catch the candlelight at eye level. "I want my parties to be fun and also for people to feel at ease," she says. "That's the key."

221

Opposite page: Graham's cutting garden features rows of poppies, sweet peas, dahlias, foxgloves, and more, all of which she uses in her arrangements.

This page: New Dawn climbing roses scale the summer home overlooking Nantucket Sound.
Opposite page: Rocking chairs on the porch offer the perfect perch for taking in views of the water.

verdant escapes

There's something endlessly seductive about the notion of disappearing to a place where worries slip away, replaced instead by a blithe, carefree bliss. These properties embrace that allure with aplomb, providing respite in settings that are inspiring, soulful, and sublime.

Opposite page: A profusion of white blooms surround the trees lining a terrace. *Preceding page:* A lush arbor, courtyard sculpture, and delicate blooms are classical counterpoints to a rugged, mountainous view.

NATURAL CHARM In a bucolic setting that feels as much like Tuscany as California, a Texas couple create their own European-inspired family retreat.

When a Texas couple bought a small luxury spa in southern California in 2000, they moved into the previous owner's residence—a one-bedroom cottage on the property. With three children, they soon realized they needed a bigger home close to the spa, but far enough away that the children could play without disturbing guests.

On a nearby hilltop, they found a site straight out of Tuscany, with 360-degree views of vineyards and farms. Architect Michael Carbine was commissioned to build a home inspired by Villa San Michele, a 15th-century monastery-turned-hotel outside of Florence, then turned to Los Angeles designer Laurie Steichen to decorate the home's Italian-accented rooms and shaded terraces with their cache of objects and furniture. The couple had a tendency to lose their hearts to lovely antiques and already had a store-room filled to the rafters with 17th- and 18th-century treasures they'd been collecting for years on trips overseas, like the 17th-century Italian chest that mingles with vintage painted wicker furniture on the loggia. "I know where every piece came from and why we bought it," says the wife, "which makes this house feel even more special."

Opposite page: Gracefully worn antiques and faux-distressed finishes create the feel of a European villa.

This page: The landscape takes its cues from Tuscan gardens; the property overlooks lush hillsides of vineyards and farms. *Opposite page:* On the loggia, painted wicker furniture is paired with a 17th-century Italian chest.

This page: The glittering pool is accented by antique statuary, distressed planters, and a large fountain.
Opposite page: The homeowners often invite spa guests up to their home for cocktails on the loggia, which inevitably turns into a tour of the house and its captivating contents.

THE PERFECT SETTING Julia Berger revisits the majestic landscape of her family's storied Northern California estate.

Situated on 74 acres in Northern California, the Green Gables estate—an Arts and Crafts masterpiece designed by architects Henry and Charles Greene—was built in 1911 as a summer escape for San Francisco's prominent Fleishhacker family. Since then, it has hosted five generations of extended clan members, among them Julia Berger. "Green Gables was a big playground for me as a child," recalls Berger, the founder of Julia B., a purveyor of exquisitely monogrammed fine linens. Berger traces her love affair with textiles back to the days she spent delving into the "cavernous" linen closet in the main house. And there was even more to explore outdoors, from manicured gardens to shaded patios to a grand Roman reflecting pool—a masterpiece of architecture and landscape design, completed in 1922, that was inspired by the grounds of the Villa Aldobrandini near Rome.

Berger recently returned to Green Gables to host an alfresco luncheon for family and friends. "What's wonderful about this place is that there are so many spots for entertaining," she says. "We can have cocktails at the top of the Roman pool or picnic on the lawn with a bottle of wine. As the Italian proverb states, *A tavola non s'invecchia*: One does not grow old at the table."

235

Opposite page: In a shaded area by the lily pond, a table set for an alfresco lunch includes vintage enameled-metal chairs that have been at Green Gables for more than five decades. *Following pages:* The property's majestic Roman Pool.

SPIRIT OF SUMMER In Newport, Rhode Island, one family's new generation gives their ancestral retreat an infustion of color, style, and good cheer.

For two months every summer, one Chicago couple's colorful home in Newport, Rhode Island, comes to life. Neighbors reconnect, simple luxuries like a cup of coffee on the terrace become part of the morning routine, and kids climb beech trees and roam freely on the large lawn with their dogs. There are naps to take, martinis to drink, parties to attend, friends to see, games of flashlight tag to play after dark—all at full tilt until the season slips away and the moment comes to return to Illinois once more.

When they inherited the house, the couple turned to friend and decorator Ruthie Sommers to help them transform the home into a welcoming retreat for their own family of five while maintaining a reverence for its past. "The house is now less fancy and more fun," Sommers says. It's the perfect sensibility for a summer house: beautiful, but also blissfully carefree. "If there's sand on the floor, it's okay—we have a vacuum," says the wife. "There's no space too precious to play in."

239

Opposite page: Purple accents appear throughout the home, indoors and out—including on the terrace, which opens onto a lush, seven-acre lawn punctuated by the trees the family's children spend summers climbing.

VERDUROUS PATHS With its modern farmhouse feel, a striking new contemporary home in the Hamptons frames the beauty of nature's canvas with picture-perfect views.

When a New York–based philanthropist and art collector and her husband built their new weekend home in the Hamptons, they sought a space that was gracious, easy, modern—both indoors and out. Their last Hamptons house was a 19th-century shingled classic with many small rooms—charming, but also a bit warren-like. Their vision for the new retreat—designed with Steven Harris Architects—was a home that would resemble a series of postmodern connected barns, all on one floor. The low-slung home also connects seamlessly to the landscape in a way that's as artful as the interiors, with oversized exterior doors and windows that seemingly vanish when opened. An infinity pool visually blends into the graceful, marshy pond just beyond the homesite and a network of wild, barely tamed paths and meadows. "I am Mediterranean, so there is never enough water for me," she says.

Opposite page: A garden path is surrounded by native grasses and river birch.

An infinity pool visually blends into the graceful, marshy pond just beyond the homesite and a network of wild, barely tamed paths and meadows. "I am Mediterranean, so there is never enough water for me," says the homeowner.

This page: A solitary bench is surrounded by wildflowers. *Opposite page:* Evoking a modern barn, the cedar-shingled Hamptons home features an infinity pool surrounded by a lush pond. Like the home's interiors, the landscape features flashes of color against a soothing backdrop.

INSIDE AND OUT

A new residence is imbued with the charm of an old European country house—albeit one that sits comfortably in the midst of modern Atlanta.

To walk into a space and feel a sense of calm is a blessing of good design. "It's always a goal to create architecture that affects a person in a positive way," says architect D. Stanley Dixon, who has clearly achieved that in an Atlanta house he designed in collaboration with decorator Carolyn Malone. The clients had for many years occupied a large, traditional, and antiques-filled house. But they were ready to embrace a new start: a home with serene outdoor spaces and uncluttered interiors. The couple was drawn to the romance of the rural houses and barns they had seen on trips to the English countryside, but while they wanted their new home to have that ambience, it also needed to fit into its milieu in the heart of the city. "They definitely didn't want a theme house," Malone says, "but rather one that could exist comfortably anywhere."

Dixon retained the higgledy-piggeldy charm of country houses by incorporating a multilevel roofline and several chimneys, while imposing order with a symmetrical layout. The rooms themselves are intimate yet graciously proportioned: High ceilings and large steel casement windows welcome the light, and many of the windows and doors open onto an interior courtyard, connecting interior spaces to nature and a tranquil garden designed by landscaping firms Boxwoods and Gardenology. The effect is "calm, bright, and warm, all at the same time," says Dixon.

245

Opposite page: The wine room opens onto a garden of olive trees, thyme, and wisteria. *Following pages:* The design of the home was inspired by rural English architecture.

249

This page: Windows open onto a verdant garden. *Opposite page:* The entry leads both into the home and to a courtyard garden.

This page: The family's dogs wait on the entry porch. *Opposite page:* The covered back porch is outfitted with an antique table and inviting chairs.

LA VIE EN ROSE A charming villa on the French Riviera offers a sophisticated take on Mediterranean ease.

Fame can alter a place, changing the very things that drew people to it in the first place. But Saint-Tropez, on the French Riviera, is that rare breed of village that has managed to withstand decades of admiration without sacrificing an ounce of its native charm. These days, it is both a chic playground and a charming refuge. Such is the spirit embodied by La Violette, a villa designed by architect Piero Castellini Baldissera for a client friend.

Nestled in the hills above the Gulf of Saint-Tropez, the house is surrounded by lavender bushes, olive groves, vineyards, and pine and cypress trees, such that even in the high season it feels tranquil and protected. The serenity of the design underscores the point that this is a house that places no demands on those who sojourn there, other than to loll by the pool, unwind beneath the wisteria-covered pergola, or gather in the garden dining area, the site of festive dinners all summer long. Adding to that sense of ease is the fact that nearly every room opens directly to the outside. "The idea was to have no separation between indoors and out," says Castellini. "It is one space that flows."

Opposite page: The stucco villa is nestled into the hills above Saint-Tropez.

This page: Agapanthus and plumbago flowers encircle the dining area; beyond are orange, pomegranate, lemon, and cypress trees. *Opposite page:* The pool terrace, sheathed in Tuscan terra-cotta tile, is a seamless extension of the house.

THE POWER OF RESTRAINT With a-less-is-more approach to design, a coastal compound makes the most of its picture-perfect setting above the surf.

Patience is a virtue in most professions, but Tom Kligerman, a principal at the architecture firm Ike Kligerman Barkley in Manhattan, might wager that it is particularly rewarding in his line of work. Consider the waterfront home he recently completed for longtime clients: Set into a hill and overlooking the Atlantic, the modern Shingle-style compound Kligerman fondly refers to as "the upside-down house" represents a synthesis of ideas and designs he has been thinking about since he was a boy.

Having spent his childhood summers in Rhode Island in a home with bedrooms on the ground floor and the living spaces above, he always wanted to design his own version. "Why wouldn't you want to be above deck, so to speak? As if on a boat? No one ever said, 'Run below and see if the pirates are coming!'" he says. Kligerman was so smitten with the topsy-turvy concept that he proposed a plan to build a version years earlier for the couple, but in the Rocky Mountains. While that project never materialized, the desire to execute it only intensified. "When I realized the land for the new home sloped down to the water, I reintroduced the design because so many of the original ideas translated," he says. For the couple, taking full advantage of the water views made perfect sense.

Respecting a region's architectural integrity figures largely in Kligerman's work. He calls this project his "experiment" with a traditional New England house. "The big question was, how modern can I make it without losing the character that makes it so special?" It turns out that time-honored sloped rooflines and double-hung windows play well with reductive versions of moldings and trims—and when there are 270-degree views from the breakfast nook, who needs a widow's walk on the roof? Kligerman framed up the space based on views of the water, cliffs, and woods, drawing up sight lines on a nautical chart before testing them out on the actual property. "Everything is meant to echo where the sky meets the water and the water meets the land," he says.

Opposite page: The views unfold from the doorway of the cedar-clad entry. *Following pages:* A restored guesthouse retains its early 20th-century character opposite the gunite pool.

BLURRING THE LINES Airy interiors seamlessly blend with the great outdoors in a soothing oasis in Malibu.

"Malibu is a place where people live out their fantasies," says interior designer Martyn Lawrence Bullard. For his clients, that fantasy was a departure from the usual gated estate on a bluff overlooking the Pacific waves. "My wife and I wanted to live in a neighborhood where our three kids and their friends could hang out at home and play in a yard," says the husband of the couple's 14,000-square-foot home set above a ravine near the rocky cliffs of Point Dune Beach. "So we sacrificed an ocean view."

The husband focused on the outdoor spaces, working with landscape architect James Hyatt, to bring in palms and succulents from around the world, including a rare drago tree and fragrant plumeria. They created a lushly planted tropical hideaway complete with its own aquatic vistas: a koi pond and water feature in the Balinese-inspired front courtyard, and a teak-decked pool and spa surrounded by palms and succulents in the back. Both gardens are visible from the living room, a nautical-yet-refined space redesigned by architect Doug Burdge to include 12-foot-tall steel French doors that give the impression of sitting in a gazebo. "People talk about indoor-outdoor living, but if you think about the outdoors last, you discount it," he says. "We wanted barefooted sophistication. You walk in here and you're in another world."

Opposite page: The pool is a tropical oasis surrounded by palms.

This page: French doors open to gardens on both sides of the living room. *Opposite page:* An outdoor kitchen for easy entertaining is adjacent to the pergola-covered dining table.

GREEN ACRES *While shopping in Paris, designer Nancy Braithwaite and her husband were so taken with François-Xavier Lalanne's sheep sculptures that they bought one for their Atlanta garden. It must have looked lonely on the lawn, because as a gift, each secretly ordered one more for the other. The little flock now adds whimsy to the rectilinear garden.*

Opposite page: A pared-to-perfection home in Atlanta combines classic farmhouse style with contemporary elegance, including a small flock of Lalanne-designed sheep on the velvety lawn.

PERFECT PATINA Just blocks from the Pacific, an Andalusian-style home in Montecito is infused with the warmth and spirit of old-world Europe.

The California-born designer Richard Hallberg has been fascinated by all things Andalusian since his first visit at age 15. "I always thought: How can I live in L.A. and Spain at the same time?" he says. His stateside design business prevents a literal move, so this transportive three-bedroom getaway in Montecito, just a seven-minute walk to the beach, is his antidote. It has all the elements of a cinematic Spanish *finca*: 24-inch-thick walls, antique-stone floors, four fireplaces, multiple courtyards, and a tile roof. "If I'm here, I'm on vacation," he says. "It's like I've left the States."

The house was built in 1926 by another American besotted with Spain. Noted Santa Barbara architect Lutah Maria Riggs designed it for herself. "She called it Clavelitos, which means 'little carnations,'" says Hallberg. But by the time Hallberg bought it, after three years of searching for the perfect house, Clavelitos had fallen into a Grey Gardens—esque state of disrepair, with overgrown grounds that looked, as he puts it, like "a crazy tropical nightmare." Still, it had the right bones.

Outside, he enhanced the grounds with a pool and terrace—complete with a rare 16th-century stone lion presiding over the lawn—where he hosts parties. The oaks were already there, but Hallberg planted mature olive trees, as well as sheltering *Ficus nitida* hedges that have grown to be 14 feet tall. He kept the garden purposefully green, selecting indigenous plantings that also flourish in Andalusia—but no colorful flowers. "The house was a jewel," Hallberg says, "and I wanted to wrap it up in a green box."

267

Opposite page: Fourteen-foot-tall hedges surround the pool and terrace, which features a 16th-century stone lion and a lily pad—laden water garden.

This page: A hedge-lined gravel path leads to a simple stone table. *Opposite page:* For the courtyard steps, Hallberg imported antique French tiles in colors ranging from terra-cotta to blue-gray. Columns and swaths of gravel form a walkway through the garden.

The house was a jewel, and I wanted to wrap it up in a green box," Hallberg says. "If I'm here, I'm on vacation. It's like I've left the States."

269

TIME AND AGAIN For two San Francisco design luminaries, a cozy Montecito cottage has provided a stable respite from the buzz of city life.

The sweet scent of osmanthus blossoms hovers in the abundant gardens that surround the Montecito bungalow of San Francisco interior designer Suzanne Tucker and her husband and business partner of more than 30 years, Timothy Marks. The lush grounds—landscaped with California oak, redwood, magnolia, and olive trees; blooming jasmine and citrus; and a dramatic 30-foot-tall white bird-of-paradise—frame their very private and serene world. "It's our own secret garden," Tucker says, "with incredible views of the Santa Ynez Mountains." In the designer's expert hands, the sunny cottage, just 1,300 square feet, is a luxurious cocoon, with welcoming armchairs beside a handsome fireplace, lusciously draped four-post beds, and a relaxed color scheme of pale hues—restrained decor that emphasizes the home's peaceful, meditative quality.

Built in the 1930s, the structure was originally a tractor garage and housing for workers of a local family's extensive lemon orchards. The landscaping reminded Tucker of what the Montecito region, where she grew up, resembled before many of its fruit groves were sold and subdivided for development. The property had been converted into a weekend retreat by the late designer James Northcutt, who transformed its old staff quarters into this charming cottage and landscaped the grounds with a pool and terrace. In 1996, the couple acquired it as their vacation home. "It's all we need to be very happy," Tucker says.

Opposite page: The pale pink stucco of a Montecito weekend home was inspired by the palette of California's historic haciendas. Framed by olive trees, the entrance faces a tranquil garden where rosemary, gardenias, strawberry guavas, and a podocarpus tree thrive throughout the seasons.

This page: Chaises and kumquat trees in terra-cotta planters enliven the pool deck. *Opposite page:* On the loggia, a pillar-capital table base is a striking centerpiece for outdoor dining.

PATH TO PARADISE The humble charm and character of a 17th-century cottage in the German countryside captures the imagination of a designer with a passion for history.

Peter Nolden had lived several other lives before he became a much-sought-after interior designer. First he was a nurse, then he was a teacher, and then, in his 30s, he went back to school to become a psychologist. It was only when he landed in the Hanseatic harbor city of Hamburg in his early 40s that he allowed himself to make a career of his lifelong love: collecting beautiful old objects and furniture.

He found his weekend home in Schleswig-Holstein, a rural area of dandelion-yellow rapeseed fields, farms, reed-thatched homes, and raw coastline just over an hour's drive north of Hamburg. The renovated 17th-century farmhouse, set on three acres of overgrown land, was built on a man-made island in the region's floodplains just 10 miles from the North Sea. "I immediately fell in love with the original stone floors," says Nolden. "That's what I love the most—finding a house that is 'in its own juice,' as they say in French, then diving into its history as a starting point. Of course we all want modern infrastructure, hot water, and heat, but I like to walk into a historic house and find myself in the age that it was built." In the gardens, a sense of history permeates, as well. Sinuous benches with a timeworn patina beckon, while architectural accents and mismatched plantings evoke a bygone era.

275

Opposite page: The garden is planted with rhododendrons, strawberries, and climbing roses. *Following pages:* A farmer herds sheep in front of the 17th-century thatched-roof farmhouse that serves as designer Peter Nolden's weekend house in rural northern Germany.

TROPICAL GLAMOUR With Continental flair and exotic flourishes, a 1920s Palm Beach villa sparkles under the bright Florida sunshine.

When an American diplomat and his wife bought this grand home on Palm Beach's waterfront nearly 30 years ago, the craze for British country-house decoration was at its height. The massive Palladian edifice, which stands in contrast with the Mediterranean- and Regency-style structures that dominate the renowned stretch of real estate, was designed by prominent Palm Beach architect John Volk in the 1920s for an heir to the Kroger grocery fortune. "It felt terribly dated," the wife recalls when they first laid eyes on it. Since then, she has turned the residence, with its Fitzgerald-era provenance, into a fantasia that reflects both the uniquely haute-American vibe of Palm Beach and the timeless classicism to which she is instinctively drawn. The house has a sense of permanence without seeming mired in history—a mix of classic, contemporary, and exotic elements that combine to give it a timeless quality. "You edit, you refine, you redefine," she says. "You never stop, which is what makes the house feel alive."

Opposite page: The garden, created in collaboration with Mario Nievera, is imbued with an old-world spirit.

This page: A grand staircase leads to the enchanting poolside area. *Opposite page:* Inlaid seashells embellish the loggia's French doors.

LAND OF ENCHANTMENT On their oceanfront property in the Hamptons, a couple creates a veritable Eden with bountiful plantings and exuberant blooms.

After renting Woody House for eight years, philanthropist Katharine Rayner and her husband William, a former magazine executive and painter, purchased the cottage and 12 surrounding acres in 1988. They were charmed by the house's simplicity—it was originally the guest quarters of a grand estate owned by Pan American World Airways founder Juan Trippe—and its setting on a windswept isthmus between the Atlantic Ocean and a saltwater lagoon. Since then, without a master plan or pesticides, and inspired by her visits to legendary estates in England, Italy, India, and Iran, she has transformed a forest of black pines into an enchanting folly.

Visitors reach the cottage's front door via a series of slightly pitched whimsical garden "rooms" strung together by winding paths. A revolving gate leads to the White Garden, where the garden beds—reminiscent of Vita Sackville-West's Sissinghurst Castle in England—overflow with bleeding hearts, foxgloves, Japanese anemones, and roses. To protect her plants from wind and salt-air exposure, she borrowed another idea from Sissinghurst, creating a series of garden rooms enclosed with walls of dense yews and boxwoods. A Mediterranean-inspired path runs past an oak arbor, where an Arts and Crafts–style fountain pays homage to the iconic horticulturist Gertrude Jekyll. In the dreamy Mughal Garden, plants are based on the 16th-century memoirs of Babur, founder of the Mughal Empire, and a narrow canal filled with water lilies and lotuses culminates in a pavilion surrounded by a profusion of roses.

The most recent addition to the property is the pool garden. Nearby, sculptor Simon Verity and his partner, architect Martha Finney, created a fanciful grotto based on Florence's Villa Medicea di Castello. Constructed using tufa, seashells, quartz, and limestone, the handcrafted folly trickles with water and dazzles at night. "We work with Mother Nature here," says head gardener John Hill, referring to the elements and, perhaps, also to the garden's visionary creator.

Opposite page: Dogs roam freely throughout, chasing butterflies, rabbits, and birds—finches, doves, and plovers. "You think you're at the symphony sometimes," says John Hill, the head gardener. Here, his Chesapeake Bay retriever enters a butterfly-patterned gate.

This page: An overview of the gardens, looking toward a coastal lagoon, reveals a combination of structure and whimsy. *Opposite page:* The Hoops—a series of arbors blanketed with five types of roses—evoke Claude Monet's gardens at Giverny.

This page: A small bridge in the Mughal Garden spans a pond filled with water lilies and tortoises. *Opposite page:* A curved tufa-stone fountain in the Italian Garden incorporates oak benches for reflection; an arbor of espaliered pear trees provides shade with elaborate yew hedges. A garden path includes stone walls inspired by Gertrude Jekyll's designs.

"We work with Mother Nature here," says head gardener John Hill, referring to the elements and, perhaps, also to the garden's visionary creator.

287

Proceding pages: Fantastical shell chairs reign over the garden pool area. An Edwin Lutyens–style garden bench is positioned at the base of a stairway leading to the Mediterranean Garden. Handrails here and throughout the property are crafted from fallen tree branches collected after storms. *This page:* A table is set for a summer lunch by the pool. *Opposite page:* Sculptor Simon Verity and architect Martha Finney fashioned a fanciful grotto from tufa stone, seashells, limestone, and quartz.

PHOTOGRAPHY

Page 4: Photography © James Merrell, interior design by Cathy Kincaid, produced by David M. Murphy

Page 6: Photography © Alexandre Bailhache, interior design by Marston Luce, produced by Carolyn Englefield

Page 265: Photography © Simon Upton, interior design by Nancy Braithwaite, architecture by James Means and Norman Davenport Askins, landscape design by William T. Smith and Associates

IN FULL BLOOM: Pages 8-19, front cover flap: Photography © Victoria Pearson, produced by Clinton Smith

PICTURE PERFECT: Pages 20-25: Photography © Max Kim-Bee, interior design by Mark D. Sikes, produced by Carolyn Englefield

FORCE OF NATURE: Pages 26-31: Photography © Roger Davies, interior design by Christina Rottman, architecture by Bob Easton, landscape design by Douglas Hoerr, floral design by Laura Sangas, produced by Carolyn Englefield

FRENCH ACCENT: Pages 32-39: Photography © Roger Davies, interior design by Anthony Baratta, architecture by Steve Giannetti, landscape architecture by Perry Guillot

AMERICAN BEAUTY: Pages 40-45: Photography © Max Kim-Bee, interior design by Frank De Biasi, architecture by Leonard Woods, landscape design by Innocent & Webel, produced by Carolyn Englefield

ESTATE OF GRACE: Pages 2, 46-53: Photography © Max Kim-Bee, landscape architecture by Charles Stick, produced by Carolyn Englefield

A SENSE OF PLACE: Pages 54-57: Photography © Matthew Millman, interior design by Paul Vincent Wiseman and Brenda Mickel, architecture by Pacific Peninsula Group, landscape design by Thomas Klope Associates

PURE BEAUTY: Pages 58-63: Photography © John M. Hall, landscape design by Madison Cox and Dan Kiley

EXOTIC INFLUENCES: Pages 64-69: Photography © James Merrell, interior design by Emily Summers, architecture by Marc Appleton, produced by David M. Murphy

TEXAS TRIUMPH: Page 71: Photography © Victoria Pearson, interior design by J. Randall Powers, architecture by Drew S. Wommack, landscape design by Johnny Steele, produced by David M. Murphy

PARTY READY: Pages 72-75: Photography © Lisa Romerein

PERSONAL SCRAPBOOK: Pages 76-79: Photography © Francesco Lagnese, interior design by Thomas O'Brien and Dan Fink, produced by Robert Rufino

PAST PERFECT: Pages 80-85: Photography ©

Max Kim-Bee, architecture by Hamady Architects, landscape design by Doyle Herman Design Associates, produced by Carolyn Englefield

PARADISE FOUND: Pages 86-87, 163: Photography © James Merrell, interior design by David Kleinberg, produced by David M. Murphy

PEACEFUL KINGDOM: Page 90-99: Photography © Max Kim-Bee, interior design by Ann Holden, architecture by Warner Group Architects, produced by Carolyn Englefield

MASTER CLASS: Pages 1, 100-105: Photography © Thomas Loof, interior and landscape design by John Saladino, produced by Carolyn Englefield

GRACE NOTES: Pages 106-109: Photography © Richard Powers, interior design by Ohara Davies-Gaetano

RETURN TO EDEN: Pages 110-115: Photography © Max Kim-Bee, interior design by Nicola and Elda Fabrizio,mproduced by Carolyn Englefield

A GRAND PLAN: Pages 116-119: Photography © Max Kim-Bee, interior design by Richard Hallberg, architecture by Appleton & Associates, landscape design by Clark and White

INDEPENDENT SPIRIT: Pages 120-123: Photography © Bjorn Wallender, interior design by Kate Cordsen, landscape design by River-End Landscaping, produced by Carolyn Englefield & Anne Foxley

STAR QUALITY: Pages 124-127: Photography © Mali Azima, interior design by Melanie Turner, architecture by Pak Heydt & Associates, landscape design by Land Plus Associates, produced by David M. Murphy

PERFECTLY SUITED: Pages 128-131: Photography © Max Kim-Bee, interior design by Tara Shaw, architecture by Barry Fox, landscape design by Byron Adams and Wanda Metz Chase, producec by Carolyn Englefield

SUNSHINE STATE: Pages 132-137: Photography © Bjorn Wallender, interior design by Lou Marotta, produced by Carolyn Englefield

AMERICAN REVIVAL: Pages 139-143: Photography © Max Kim-Bee, interior design by Victoria Hagan, architecture by Oscar S hamamian, landscape design by Doyle Herman Design Associates, produced by Carolyn Englefield

PACIFIC PARADISE: Pages 144-149: Photography © Roger Davies, interior design by Hutton Wilkinson, produced by Carolyn Englefield

CALIFORNIA COOL: Pages 150-153: Photography © Laura Resen, interior design by Greg Stewart, Principal at Odada (Orlando Diaz-Azcuy Design Associates), produced by Carolyn Englefield

SIMPLY SERENE: Pages 154-159: Photography © Chris Little & Joe Little, interior design by Rozanne Jackson, architecture and landscape design by Marieanne Khoury-Vogt & Erik Vogt

OUT EAST: Pages 160, 164-167: Photography

© Quentin Bacon, interior design by Quinn Pofahl, architecture by Fred Smith, produced by Carolyn Englefield

ROOM TO ROAM: Pages 168-175: Photography © Lisa Romerein, interior design by Steve and Brooke Giannetti, architecture by Steve Giannetti, landscape design by Steve Giannetti and Margaret Grace, Grace Design Associates

SUMMER SPLENDOR: Pages 176-179: Photography © Emily Followill, produced by Mario Lopez-Cordero

ART OF ARRIVAL: Page 180: Photography © Max Kim-Bee, interior design by Beverly Field, architecture by Richardson Roberston III, produced by Carolyn Englefield

HAMPTONS HIDEAWAY: Pages 182-185: Photography © Max Kim-Bee; interior design by Kelli Ford and Kirsten Fitzgibbons, architecture by Peter Pennoyer, landscape design by Deborah Nevins and Associates, produced by Carolyn Englefield

LONDON CALLING: Page 187: Photography © Stephan Julliard, interior design by Jean-Louis Deniot

SWEET CAROLINA: Pages 188-191: Photography © James Merrell, interior design by Elizabeth Locke, produced by David M. Murphy

GEORGIAN REVIVAL: Pages 193-195: Photography © Bjorn Wallender, interior design by Suzanne Kasler, architecture by Madison Spencer, landscape design by Rieley & Associates, produced by Robert Rufino

CLASSIC CHARM: Pages 196-203: Photography © James Merrell, interior design by Cathy Kincaid, architecture by J. Wilson Fuqua, landscape design by Paul Fields, produced by David M. Murphy

ROMANTIC BY NATURE: Pages 204-207: Photography © Roger Davies, interior and landscape design by Mark D. Sikes, produced by Carolyn Englefield

EASY BREEZY: Pages 208-211: Photography © Victoria Pearson, interior design by Kathryn M. Ireland, produced by Carolyn Englefield

GRAND TRADITIONS: Pages 213-215: Photography © William Waldron, interior design by David Kleinberg, architecture and landscape design by Kevin Murphy, styled by Olga Naiman

HIGH IMPACT: Pages 216-219: Photography © Joshua McHugh, interior design by Nick Olsen, produced by Robert Rufino

A BOUNTY OF BLOOMS: Pages 220-223: Photography © Quentin Bacon

NATURAL CHARM: Pages 224-233: Photography © Max Kim-Bee, interior design by Laurie Steichen, architecture by M. Carbine Restorations, produced by Carolyn Englefield

THE PERFECT SETTING: Pages 234-237: Photography © Laura Resen, produced by Dayle Wood

292

SPIRIT OF SUMMER: Page 238: Photography © William Waldron, interior design by Ruthie Sommers, produced by Carolyn Englefield

VERDUROUS PATHS: Pages 240-243: Photography © Max Kim-Bee, interior design by Luis Bustamante, architecture by Steven Harris, landscape design by David Kelly, produced by Pilar Crespi

INSIDE AND OUT: Pages 244-251: Photography © Annie Schlecter, interior design by Carolyn Malone, architecture by D. Stanley Dixon, landscape design by Boxwoods and Gardenology, produced by David M. Murphy

LA VIE EN ROSE: Pages 252-255: Photography © Alexandre Bailhache, interior and landscape design by Piero Castellini Baldissera, produced by Carolyne Englefield

THE POWER OF RESTRAINT: Pages 256-259: Photography © William Waldron, interior design by Mia Jung, architecture by Thomas A. Kligerman, landscape design by Kris Horiuchi

BLURRING THE LINES: Pages 260-263: Photography © Roger Davies, interior design by Martyn Lawrence Bullard, architecture by Doug Burdee, landscape design by James Hyatt, produced by Carolyn Englefield

PERFECT PATINA: Pages 266-269: Photography © Max Kim-Bee, interior and landscape design by Richard Hallberg, produced by Carolyn Englefield

TIME AND AGAIN: Pages 270-273: Photography © Roger Davies, interior design by Suzanne Tucker and Timothy Marks, produced by Carolyn Englefield

PATH TO PARADISE: Pages 274-277: Photography © Andreas von Einsiedel, interior design by Peter Holden, landscape design by Clemens Zylka

TROPICAL GLAMOUR: Pages 278-281: Photography © Bjorn Wallender, produced by Carolyn Englefield

LAND OF ENCHANTMENT: Pages 282-291: Photography © Tria Giovan

INDEX